# Dear Parents:

Congratulations! Your child is taking the first steps on an exciting journey. The destination? Independent reading!

**STEP INTO READING**® will help your child get there. The program offers five steps to reading success. Each step includes fun stories and colorful art or photographs. In addition to original fiction and books with favorite characters, there are Step into Reading Non-Fiction Readers, Phonics Readers and Boxed Sets, Sticker Readers, and Comic Readers—a complete literacy program with something to interest every child.

## Learning to Read, Step by Step!

**Ready to Read   Preschool–Kindergarten**
• big type and easy words • rhyme and rhythm • picture clues
For children who know the alphabet and are eager to begin reading.

**Reading with Help   Preschool–Grade 1**
• basic vocabulary • short sentences • simple stories
For children who recognize familiar words and sound out new words with help.

**Reading on Your Own   Grades 1–3**
• engaging characters • easy-to-follow plots • popular topics
For children who are ready to read on their own.

**Reading Paragraphs   Grades 2–3**
• challenging vocabulary • short paragraphs • exciting stories
For newly independent readers who read simple sentences with confidence.

**Ready for Chapters   Grades 2–4**
• chapters • longer paragraphs • full-color art
For children who want to take the plunge into chapter books but still like colorful pictures.

**STEP INTO READING**® is designed to give every child a successful reading experience. The grade levels are only guides; children will progress through the steps at their own speed, developing confidence in their reading.

Remember, a lifetime love of reading starts with a single step!

*For my voting nieces—Stephanie, Miriam, Naomi,*
*Isabelle, Rebecca, and Julie —M.K.*

**Acknowledgments:** Grateful thanks to my esteemed editor, Heidi Kilgras, with whom I've joyfully worked for over two decades. Thanks also to Linda Lopata, Director of Interpretation and Visitor Services at the National Susan B. Anthony Museum & House in Rochester, New York, for her guidance.

Visit us on the Web!
StepIntoReading.com
rhcbooks.com

Educators and librarians, for a variety of teaching tools, visit us at RHTeachersLibrarians.com

*Library of Congress Cataloging-in-Publication Data*
Names: Kulling, Monica, author. | Plenzke, Maike, illustrator.
Title: Susan B. Anthony: her fight for equal rights / by Monica Kulling; illustrated by Maike Plenzke.
Description: New York: Random House, [2020] | Series: Step into reading. Step 2
Identifiers: LCCN 2019010391 (print) | LCCN 2019012047 (ebook) | ISBN 978-0-593-11982-2 (trade pbk.) | ISBN 978-0-593-11983-9 (lib. bdg.) | ISBN 978-0-593-11984-6 (ebook)
Subjects: LCSH: Anthony, Susan B. (Susan Brownell), 1820–1906—Juvenile literature. | Feminists—United States—Biography—Juvenile literature. | Suffragists—United States—Biography—Juvenile literature. | Women's rights—United States—History—Juvenile literature. | Feminism—United States—History—Juvenile literature.
Classification: LCC HQ1413.A55 (ebook) | LCC HQ1413.A55 K85 2020 (print)
DDC 305.42092 [B]—dc23

Printed in the United States of America
10 9 8 7 6 5 4 3 2 1

This book has been officially leveled by using the F&P Text Level Gradient™ Leveling System.

# Susan B. Anthony
## Her Fight for Equal Rights

by Monica Kulling
illustrated by Maike Plenzke

Random House 🏠 New York

Today,
girls can grow up
to be anything
they want.

They can be
rocket scientists,
race car drivers,
or even the president!

In the early 1800s,
women did not have
the same rights as men.
They could not own land.

Married women
could not keep
the money they earned.

Black women had
the fewest rights of all.
Most black women
were enslaved.

Women could not change the laws to make life better.

They could not vote.
Many brave women
fought for this right.
Susan B. Anthony may have
fought the hardest.

Susan Brownell Anthony
was born on
February 15, 1820,
in Adams, Massachusetts.

Susan loved school.

She was eager to learn.

Susan's teacher
would not teach her
long division.
"Girls don't need to
know that," he said.

So Susan's father
took his children
out of school.
They would learn at home.

Susan grew up
to be a teacher.
But she was paid
far less than a man
doing the same job.

"It's not fair!" she said.

Susan quit teaching.

She gave her heart
to the fight
for human rights.

She worked with
the Underground Railroad.
This group helped
enslaved people
escape to freedom.

Susan wanted to
use her voice for change.
But at one meeting,
the women were told
to "listen and learn."

Susan was angry.

"I am a citizen, too!"

Susan met

Elizabeth Cady Stanton.

Elizabeth was fighting
for women's rights, too.
They joined forces.

Elizabeth had to
stay at home
with her children.

She wrote speeches
that Susan gave
to crowds across America.

In November 1872,
Susan did something daring.

# She voted in the election for president!

Susan had told
women across America
to vote, too.

Many of them did.

She wrote to Elizabeth,

"I have gone and done it!"

Susan was arrested
and put on trial!
The judge said
Susan must pay a fine.

"I will not pay
one dollar!"
replied Susan.
And she never did.

Susan B. Anthony fought
for women's rights
for over fifty years.

She died in 1906.
But Susan was sure
that one day,
women would be
allowed to vote.

She was right.

The law changed

in 1920.

Her fight was worth it!